Original title:
Oranges in the Sun

Copyright © 2025 Creative Arts Management OÜ
All rights reserved.

Author: Seraphina Caldwell
ISBN HARDBACK: 978-1-80586-237-6
ISBN PAPERBACK: 978-1-80586-709-8

The Dance of the Golden Fruit

In a bowl they do jiggle, bright and round,
A citrusy party, with laughter abound.
They roll off the table, a slippery spree,
Chasing each other, oh-so-giggly!

With a twist and a twirl, they start to sway,
Dancing in rhythm, come join the play.
One slips on a peel, goes spinning around,
Lands in a smoothie, oh what a sound!

Glimpses of Sun-Drenched Bliss

On a picnic blanket, bright and warm,
Zesty smiles escape, a fruity charm.
A bite brings a squirt, oh what a mess,
Sun-kissed giggles, who could guess!

The ants march in, a tiny parade,
With their own plans, none are afraid.
They join in the fun, a scrumptious line,
Who knew a snack could be so divine!

Radiant Journeys Through Citrus Groves

Bouncing through orchards, zest in the air,
Chasing the breeze, without a care.
They stop for a chat with a bumblebee,
Who buzzes along, 'Come dance with me!'

With every bright swing, laughter sets free,
Fruity friends tangled, like a wild marquee.
They roll down the hill, a merry descent,
Landing in puddles of bright sweetness sent!

Beneath a Sky of Juicy Gold

Under a canopy, so rich and bold,
Silhouettes of joy, stories unfold.
They sit on the branches, a playful band,
Sharing their secrets, oh so unplanned!

With sunshine dripping, they gleefully laugh,
Hatching grand schemes, oh what a gaffe.
They leap and they bounce, high in the light,
A citrus cloud party, what a delight!

The Glint of Citrus Under Bright Canopy

In a grove of laughter, fruits do sway,
Bouncing like kids who forgot to play.
Lemons giggle, oranges wear shades,
While limes plan pranks in leafy cascades.

With every sunbeam, a zesty jest,
Citric comedians at their very best.
The trees are the stage, the breeze takes a bow,
As fruit and foliage throw a wild pow-wow.

Gleaming Treasures of the Orchard

Adventurous grins on fruit-filled trees,
Making mischief like summer's breeze.
A grapefruit slips and rolls away,
While a cheeky tangerine laughs all day.

Juggling peels, they put on a show,
Citrusy clowns in a sunlit glow.
With zesty giggles, they bounce and cheer,
A fruity festival is drawing near.

Sun-Drenched Delicacies Await

Bright spheres glisten in the warm embrace,
Fruitful jesters vying for a race.
Ripe ones boast, claiming they're the best,
While their pals peel away in jest.

In this garden giggle, come take a taste,
Life's a party, with no hint of haste.
Zesty bites and laughter collide,
Join in the fun, let joy be your guide.

The Palette of Nature's Sunshine

A swirl of colors in the golden glow,
Fruits are the actors in nature's show.
With puns and jests, they lighten hearts,
Painting smiles with all their arts.

Nature's humor written on each skin,
Wisecracking berries making us grin.
Under the canopy, the humor's free,
Join in the jest, be wild and carefree.

The Vibrant Dance of Peel and Pith

In the garden, fruits jiggle,
Bouncing on limbs, oh what a giggle.
Peels fly off in a grand parade,
While pithy jokes serenely invade.

The zest comes out with a silly grin,
As squirrels dance, trying to fit in.
Funny faces on the juicy spheres,
Spreading laughter, igniting cheers.

Tangy Light Through Leafy Canopies

Golden globes hide in leafy nests,
Sunlight giggles, it's on a quest.
Shadows bounce, making a show,
With tangy giggles, it steals the glow.

The branches sway, a cheeky tune,
As the fruit dances, under the moon.
Nature whispers secrets, oh so sweet,
In this circus of flavor, what a treat!

Flame-Flecked Citrus Coalescence

A riot of color in the warm breeze,
Flames tickle fruit with utmost ease.
Peeled laughter echoes in the air,
As zestful spirits dance without a care.

Fruits collide in a vibrant game,
Rolling and tumbling, looking for fame.
They trip and tumble, oh what a sight,
Their citrus humor sparkles bright.

Nature's Nectar Against the Horizon

As daylight fades, a fruity jam,
Juicy fades dance, oh look at them!
Nature chuckles, in colors so grand,
Crafting laughter, its master plan.

The horizon glows with playful delight,
Squeezed out giggles, ready to ignite.
With every laugh, and every fun spin,
A tasty treat as dusk pinches in.

Aromatic Echoes of the Orchard

In a grove where giggles grow,
Fruit hangs low, in neat row,
Bees buzz with a cheeky cheer,
Dancing dreams are always near.

Lemonade rivers, tart and sweet,
Sunlight makes every bite a treat,
Squirrels in shades of bright yellow,
Join the feast, oh, what a fellow!

A jester pulls a fruity prank,
Hiding pears in a muddy tank,
Laughter rolls like a playful wave,
In this orchard, joy is brave.

The harvest brings a silly spree,
Juggling lemons like a glee,
With every twist and flip they find,
Life's just citrus, intertwined.

Colorful Days of Tangy Delight

Waking up with zestful flair,
Breakfast spread is quite the dare,
Tangerines on toast, oh my!
Could there be a better pie?

Mango hats upon our heads,
Fruit salad in the flower beds,
Balloons tied to grapefruits bright,
Floating high, a silly sight.

Sticky fingers, giggling bunch,
Squeezing juice, let's have a crunch,
Lemon peels on a wild slide,
Racing fruits, the fun we ride.

Fruity jokes around the park,
Whispers of a citrus lark,
Colorful days, we're here to play,
In the orchard, come what may!

The Warmth Behind the Peel

Beneath the skin, a sweetness hides,
Tickling taste buds like merry rides,
Banana slips and citrus spins,
In this world, the laughter wins.

Kumquats toss like bright confetti,
Bouncing off from graines, so petty,
Pineapples wear their hats so grand,
In this fruity, funny band.

Underneath the orange tree,
Squirrels share the jubilee,
Chasing tales with tangy glee,
Beneath the warmth, just let it be.

Every nibble, every bite,
Serves a sprinkle of pure delight,
Peels that slip and laughter's call,
In this warmth, we're having a ball!

Dance of Sunlit Treasures

In the garden, fruits do prance,
Dancers twirling in a chance,
Papaya pirouettes with grace,
Mango laughs, a sunny face.

A fruit fiesta in full bloom,
Every shade dispels the gloom,
Grapefruit spins a sassy tale,
With every nibble, hear the wail.

Fruity friends, what a relief,
Squeezing juice but never grief,
Connecting laughter, sunshine beams,
Plucking joy from all our dreams.

Grapes on vines form a conga line,
Tasting fun, oh what a sign,
Dance of treasures, sweet and bright,
With every bite, we ignite!

The Sweetness of Warmth Captured

In the garden where giggles grow,
Fruit like jewels in a warm, bright glow.
Chasing bees with a comical dance,
Sipping sweet nectar, a sticky romance.

Laughter spills like juice on the grass,
Wobbling weighty, we all must pass.
Orange socks in the blazing light,
Tickling toes, what a silly sight!

Citrus Echoes in the Air

A cartwheel here, a slip, a slide,
Juicy smirks we cannot hide.
With zesty jokes that make us bark,
Each punchline lands like a sweet honeyed spark.

The fragrance of laughter fills the breeze,
Amidst bright echoes, we laugh with ease.
Peel away troubles, let laughter shine,
In this citrus chaos, everything's fine!

Lively Glows of Orchard Dreams

Bouncing babes on a treasure hunt,
Finding plump gold, oh what a stunt!
Swinging from branches like merry clowns,
Sticky hands and juice-stained frowns.

Bubbles burst in a fruity parade,
Whacky games in the sun, our charade.
Harvesting giggles from every tree,
We're all just kids, wild and free!

Sun-Kissed Joy from Nature's Larder

Jolly gnomes in a citrus spree,
Trolls tossing fruit with wild glee.
Under bright skies, we frolic and play,
In a citrusy whirl, we chase the day.

Puns rolling off like the sweetest zest,
Joking about our fruit-laden quest.
Lively capers and fruity surprises,
In this sunlit dance, joy never dries!

Fields Enflamed by Nature's Palette

In a field where colors collide,
Laughter blooms on every side,
Nature's fool, with paint so bright,
Can't tell day from silly night.

Sunflowers dance, quite absurd,
As a chicken flirts with a bird,
Bees wear shades and strut in style,
While the breeze just cracks a smile.

The sky throws hues like a wild show,
A canvas where all mischief flows,
In patches of joy, it's plain to see,
Today's agenda? Just let it be!

With every splash of zestful cheer,
The world looked back and said, "Oh dear!"
A farmer tried his hand at art,
Now the corn's a gallant dart.

Slices of Summer's Warmth

On sunny days, the giggles sprout,
With juicy bites that make us shout,
A picnic spread, a feast so sweet,
But watch your sandwich, it might cheat!

The squirrels sneak in, all in a line,
With tiny paws on the grapevine,
A watermelon hat is quite the sight,
As ants hold a dance party, oh what a fright!

Lemonade turns giggles into glee,
While the ice cream melts like a happy bee,
As laughter swirls through the balmy air,
Mischief brews with flair and care.

With cherries thrown like tiny grenades,
And friends who sport an array of shades,
The season slips, but we won't fret,
Because summertime's the best roulette!

Sunshine Melodies in the Orchard

In the orchard, the banter flies,
Where apples wear their dashing ties,
A chorus of laughter, sweet and bold,
Who knew fruit could have tales told?

The pears put on a jig, oh my,
While pineapples roll like a clumsy guy,
Bananas sing in a comical tune,
Under the watch of a sleepy moon.

Orange laughter fills the trees,
As squirrels chuckle with a breeze,
The twilight twirls with fruity schemes,
And everyone shares their wild dreams.

With harmony sweeter than honey's kiss,
This merry place? Pure bliss,
So raise a toast to the fruit-filled fun,
For a day well spent under the whimsical sun!

The Aroma of Daylight's Bounty

In this garden, the scents collide,
With fragrant laughter we can't hide,
Happiness blooms in every shade,
As fruit sentries parade in charades.

The basil's tickling a tomato's side,
As gardeners laugh and take a ride,
Cucumbers giggle while peas tease,
Even lettuce joins with playful ease.

Carrots wear wigs, quite the sight,
With radishes cheering, all feels right,
Herbs engage in witty debate,
While the sun watches, full of fate.

So inhale deeply, let joy resound,
In this bounty where fun is found,
Nature's giggle fest is on display,
In the aromatic light of the day!

Harvesting Rays of Joy

In a field of golden hue,
Bright laughter fills the view.
With baskets held up high,
We dance as time floats by.

Fruits tumble down with glee,
Nature's giggles all around me.
A squirrel chuckles at our plight,
As we try to catch the light.

Juicy gems in hand we clutched,
Each splash of color wildly dulched.
With sticky fingers, we decree,
This harvest surely sets us free!

So here we sit beneath the sky,
Feasting as the moments fly.
Unruly laughter, sweet delight,
In this funny, fruitful sight.

Fruitful Reflections of a Day

Beneath the trees where shadows play,
We munch on snacks, oh what a day!
With zest and joy, our spirits soar,
Who knew picking could be a chore?

In a game of tug and cheer,
Fruit flies land, then disappear.
A friend slips on a citrus peel,
Laughter erupts, what a great deal!

As juice drips down our chin with flair,
We look like we just don't care.
A picnic here feels quite absurd,
With fruity puns that are unheard.

Reflecting on this fruity spree,
Grinning wide so happily.
In the sunshine, we'll always stay,
Joyful echoes of the day.

The Glow of Juicy Delights

In a grove where flavors dance,
We twirl around in a silly trance.
Each bite bursts open with a cheer,
Here's to sweetness, loud and clear!

A fruit fight breaks out in glee,
Sticky laughter, just you and me.
Slipping on spills, oh what a jest,
A fruity feast that feels the best!

In blushing tones, the snacks do gleam,
We plot and scheme for the next dream.
With every chomp, we love and share,
Life's juicy treasures everywhere!

So raise your snacks to skies so bright,
In this quirky, wild delight.
Here's to sweetness, here's to fun,
May our laughter be never done!

Sun-Kissed Splendor

Golden rays embrace the scene,
We giggle at each fruity glean.
With cheeks like peaches, round and bright,
Frolicking in the golden light.

With every splash, we toss and play,
Our fruity bits go flying away.
We chase the juice that slips and rolls,
With laughter echoing through our souls.

Filling baskets, shiny and bold,
Tales of sweetness waiting to be told.
In this carnival of bliss we dwell,
With joy to share, all is well!

So join this romp, come and indulge,
Let's make memories that will divulge.
In sun-kissed splendor, we unite,
In fruity fun, our hearts take flight!

The Lightness of Zesty Echoes

In the market, fruits shine bright,
A jester's dance in the warm daylight.
With peels that slip and bounce away,
I chuckle at the citrus ballet.

Lemonade oceans, sweet and spry,
Lemon-lime storms in a cloudless sky.
They tease the nose with a fragrant wink,
I trip on zest, and I start to sink.

Amid the squirt and juicy cheer,
We laugh until we shed a tear.
The fruit brigade is full of fun,
Spectacles beneath the laughing sun.

Echoes of joy in every bite,
Citrus giggles on a silly flight.
With every taste, the world's a jest,
In the laughter of the fruit, we rest.

Citrus Reverie in Golden Hours

In twilight's glow, the fruits parade,
Their vibrant charm, a grand charade.
I watch them roll with silly glee,
As if they're planning a jubilee.

Limes in sunglasses, oranges grin,
They're all set for the fun to begin.
With every slice, they giggle and tease,
Transporting us to citrus-y ease.

A fruit salad with a twist of fate,
Bananas join, and they celebrate.
Dancing forks on plates collide,
In the citrus wonder, we take pride.

Oh, how they bounce, so light, yet round,
In fruity whispers, joy is found.
Golden hours filled with chuckles bright,
In this reverie, we take delight.

A Symphony of Sweetness and Brightness

A symphony plays in the orchard's heart,
Citrus notes strike a playful start.
Lemon violins and orange flutes,
Creating laughter in their colorful suits.

The peelers join in a quirky dance,
A citrus festival, a grand romance.
With each zesty note, I can't resist,
A paring knife leads to a fruity twist.

Tangerine trumpets sound delight,
As cherries giggle, launching their flight.
In this orchestra of vibrant fun,
The sweetness lingers when day is done.

Melodies burst from each daring bite,
A taste of joy, morning until night.
This symphony brings pure elation,
In fruity harmonies, my jubilation.

Beneath the Canopy of Citrus Dreams

Underneath a leafy dome,
Citrus critters find their home.
Limes lounge while lemons shout,
In this la-la land, joy dances about.

A pulpy picnic spreads with cheer,
Every slice brings a silly sneer.
While grapefruits play peek-a-boo,
The sweetness wraps us like morning dew.

Squeezed in smiles, their laughter swells,
As high above, the sunlight dwells.
In this grove where bright dreams gleam,
Life is as juicy as it may seem.

The merry buzz of life unfurls,
Beneath the trees, the laughter twirls.
In citrus dreams, we find our spark,
Together dancing in the park.

Citrus Glow at Dusk

In the garden, wobbly gnomes,
Shouted loudly, calling home.
Juicy fruits hung, round and bright,
Bouncing softly, what a sight!

Chasing shadows, giggles sound,
Slipping, sliding on the ground.
With sticky hands and cheeky grins,
We dance and dodge, let the fun begin!

Pies and struggles, what a show,
Footballs made of zest and glow.
Laughter echoes, far and near,
Sunset's glow, we've nothing to fear!

We laugh at squirrels, plotting schemes,
With citrus dreams and silly beams.
A zestful world, let's play along,
Underneath the peachy song!

Radiant Harvest Whispers

What's that smell? Oh, sticky bliss,
A harvest feast we can't dismiss.
In the field, we frolic wide,
With citrus treasures by our side.

Juice-filled battles, let's combine,
Spinning tales of silly vines.
Veering wild, we toss and play,
Underneath the blushing ray!

Splat goes a fruit, a juicy hit,
Slipping, sliding, we can't quit.
Watch out, the farmer's on a spree,
With a hat so big, it's hard to see!

Juggling fruit, what a grand show,
Face so bright, a lovely glow.
In the fields, we'll dance away,
Harvest whispers, hip-hip-hooray!

Sun-Kissed Citrus Dreams

On a whim, we take a ride,
In a cart, we'll twist and glide.
Funny faces, laughter loud,
Squeezed together, we're so proud!

Citrus hats atop our heads,
Bouncing high on fruity beds.
With cheeky grins and stickers stuck,
We brave the storms with a little luck.

Picnic plans, a feast to share,
Dancing rays, we have no care.
Let's squeeze the day and twirl about,
Silly games, that's what it's about!

Lemonade rivers, flowing bright,
Sipping deeply, pure delight.
What a dream this day has spun,
In the light, we're all just fun!

Luminous Slices at Afternoon

In the sun, we play our game,
Orchards filled with zest and fame.
Goofy slides and flying fruits,
Spitball battles with zesty roots!

Tossing peels, a sticky scene,
Who knew this could be so keen?
Rolling, laughing, oh what joy,
Our fruity kingdom, every boy!

Under trees where laughter flows,
Grinning wide as the sun glows.
With shiny smiles and citrus cheer,
We blow the world a juicy cheer!

Time to gather, time to share,
Juicy friendships blooming fair.
In the fun, let spirits zoom,
Under shimmering citrus bloom!

The Luster of Citrus Dreams

In a grove where laughter grows,
Fruit hang low, like silly shows.
Juicy jokes bounce in warm air,
Sweet zest spills from everywhere.

Bouncing balls of sunshine bright,
Citrus hats take flight at night.
Dancing squirrels in bright attire,
Slide on peels, oh what a hire!

Funny faces on each slice,
A giggle wrapped in citrus spice.
Lemonade rivers flow and swirl,
In this land where fun's a whirl.

Resplendent Gardens of Flavor

In the garden of silly dreams,
Fruit wear mustaches, it seems.
They roll around in jolly glee,
Tickled by bees, oh so free!

Lime and lemon, a quirky team,
Plotting a heist on sweet ice cream.
With every splash and zestful dive,
They laugh so hard, they barely survive!

Dancing in the dappled shade,
Fruitful pranks, a jester's parade.
Where flavors flirt and giggles pop,
In this garden, fun won't stop!

Rays of Gold Intertwine

Rays of laughter twist and twine,
In a fruit bowl, spirits shine.
Silly spoons do pirouettes,
Joy in every juicy set!

Pineapple hats and tangerine ties,
Bouncing past in fruity disguise.
Lemon peel sliding down the hill,
Giggling at a playful thrill.

Golden rays weave through the trees,
Squeezing out giggles with the breeze.
Every curve and every line,
This golden glow is truly fine!

Fields of Delight

In fields where citrus giggles flow,
Flowers chuckle, putting on a show.
Frog musicians in the sun,
Play their tunes, everyone has fun!

Dandelions join the dance,
In every breeze, a joyful chance.
Jumping beans with leaps so wide,
Tossing zest, in joy, they glide!

Bumblebees sing silly songs,
While fruit parade along in throngs.
In these fields, laughter ignites,
Fruits shine bright in warm delights!

Daylight's Gift

Daylight spills a golden hue,
Fruit giggle, wave, and coo.
With every splash of sunny light,
They bounce around with sheer delight!

Pineapple puppies, oh what fun!
Harvesting laughter, one by one.
Banana boats sail on the breeze,
Sailing past the giggling trees.

Jokes ripen on the playful vines,
In a world where joy defines.
Sunshine's gift, a fruity spree,
In every chuckle, pure jubilee!

A Festival of Zesty Light

In a world of peels and laughter,
Zestful joy rolls on the floor.
People dance with citrus masks,
Avoiding puddles, hoping for more.

Squeezed lemon laughs in a cheer,
As tangerines bounce all around.
A parrot dressed in bright attire,
Wants to join the merry sound.

Juggling fruits in bright display,
With giggles that fill the air.
Bright colors drip like pure delight,
We embrace silliness with flair.

Limes start a conga line so fast,
While grapefruits play a bongo beat.
Underneath this zesty sky,
Life feels like a fruity treat.

Savoring the Sweetness of Nature's Bounty

Fruits nestled in the sunlit tree,
Ripe and ready, what a sight!
Each bite a burst of glee,
Making every snack a delight.

Friends gather with goofy grins,
While juice drips down our chins.
In this orchard, laughter spins,
As we play like children, it begins.

Bumblebees buzz with happiness,
Chasing shadows, flying high.
Sweetness drips in glorious mess,
As we giggle and let out a sigh.

Nature's bounty, oh so fine,
We promise not to waste a slice.
With every bite, our hearts align,
In this fruity paradise, so nice.

Days of Golden Radiance

Golden globes hang in the air,
Gleaming like a disco ball.
Sunshine glistens everywhere,
Nature's party, hear the call!

A squirrel dances with delight,
Stealing treats from someone's hand.
Cheeky jumps and acrobatic flight,
One sprightly nutty band!

With sticky fingers and bright smiles,
We gather in groups that sway.
Chasing fruit for endless miles,
Our laughter echoes through the day.

As twilight drapes a golden hue,
Jokes tumble out like sprightly seeds.
In this season's sunny view,
We find joy, that's all we need.

Juicy Memories in the Breeze

In a garden where laughter reigns,
Fruits dangle like playful dreams.
Sticky hands and grassy stains,
Breezes carry our silly screams.

Bananas slip and up we go,
Spinning round like crazy tops.
Chasing shadows, moving slow,
Laughter rises, never stops.

With each bite, a memory formed,
Sweet as candy on our lips.
Sunny days, brightly adorned,
We toast with cheeky little sips.

So here we stand, side by side,
Mischief hangs in the airy space.
With juicy hearts, we take pride,
In this fruity, funny embrace.

Warmth of the Harvest

Plump and bright, they dance with cheer,
A citrus circus, drawing near.
Juggling peels with a big, wide grin,
Watch out! Here come the fruit to spin!

Socks on the trees, a fashion bold,
Each fruit a tale waiting to be told.
They tumble down, with a thud and a squish,
A sticky adventure, oh, what a wish!

Lemonade rivers, and laughter afloat,
Sunshine spilled from a juicy boat.
With zest in the air, let's play and shout,
In this fruity fiesta, we're never in doubt!

A fruit fight erupts, who will prevail?
Giggles erupt with each citrus hail.
Caught in a splash of sweet, tangy fun,
Embracing the laughter, we all are one!

Gleaming Vistas of Autumn

The trees wear crowns of bright, shiny gold,
As fruits like suns come out from the cold.
They gleam and glisten, a glorious sight,
The squirrels are plotting a fruity delight!

Chasing the shadows in a harvest game,
A jolly parade, none feeling the same.
Pies in the kitchen, wafting a tease,
With every bite, they bring us to knees!

Wonderous fall colors, a thrilling show,
Each step crunching leaves in a joyous flow.
From baskets they tumble, a comical race,
Fruits bouncing wildly, what a funny chase!

With every chuckle, the day slips away,
In the warmth of the harvest, we laugh and play.
Autumn's bright treasures, so ripe and profound,
Gather them all, hear the laughter resound!

A Tangy Morning Glow

Rise and shine, what's that scent?
A zesty wake-up, who needs a vent?
Peels in the air, a zany spree,
Dancing with breakfast, come join me!

Sticky fingers and laughter loud,
Turning breakfast into a bustling crowd.
Jars of marmalade, bright as the day,
Spreading sunshine in a comical way!

A splash of juice, on the table it lands,
Painting faces in sticky bands.
Giggles erupt as the morning unfolds,
With each sip of sweetness, the joy never grows old!

In citrus coconuts, we get lost in glee,
As the tangy adventures bring us to the sea.
Let's ride the waves of this morning cheer,
In our fruit-filled world, we hold laughter dear!

Serene Citrus Whispers

In gardens lush, where we roam and play,
A symphony of zest greets the day.
Whispers of citrus, from tree to tree,
Sharing their secrets, wild as can be!

Breezes tickle the peels with delight,
As squirrels plot pranks from morning till night.
Giggles erupt in the mellow air,
With fruits gathering to dance and to share!

Sun-kissed rounds of a playful glow,
Rolling along with a bright little show.
In the shade of the leaves, we find our bliss,
Collecting the laughter in every sweet kiss!

In this world of wonder, we leap and twirl,
As fruity companions, we spin and whirl.
Under the branches, there's always room,
For jokes and for giggles, in sweet citrus bloom!

Sweet Stories Told Under the Sky

Underneath the bright blue dome,
A fruit juggler calls it home.
With giggles and laughter all around,
They toss and dance; merriment found.

Sweet bites burst on eager tongues,
As silly songs are playfully strung.
A parade of flavors, bright and bold,
Bringing stories, silly and old.

Beneath the trees, they laugh and cheer,
The fruit magician's show brings near.
With every plop and every splash,
A sticky chaos; oh, what a crash!

Sun-kissed cheeks and brightened eyes,
As fruity tales fill the sky.
With every twist, the fun grows strong,
In our hearts, the joy belongs.

Golden Delights of Daylight

In the light of the warm sunbeam,
Citrusy giggles make us dream.
A squeezy game, a splatter here,
Creative mess, let's all cheer!

Bouncing balls of tangy glee,
Rolls of laughter, wild and free.
A slice of fun, a juicy grin,
As sunny playtime now begins.

The sun smiles down with golden rays,
Each burst of laughter, bright displays.
With zest and zing and silly roles,
Together we dance, heart and souls.

In citrus shades, our spirits sip,
And pranksters take a daring trip.
A sunlit feast of laughs and cheer,
Golden joys, we hold them dear.

In the Glow of Juicy Wonder

Glowing goods on a bumpy ride,
A fruit cart wobbles side to side.
With squeezy tales and sticky hands,
A fruity carnival that never ends.

With every bite, a giggle roars,
As flavors dance behind closed doors.
Eager kids chase drops of zest,
In this world, we laugh the best.

In laughter's glow, the colors blend,
A chattering joy that's hard to end.
Squeezed together like a playful bunch,
In the glow of laughter, we munch.

With each bright hue, a game anew,
Tickling our toes, a joy so true.
Let's swirl and twirl on the green grass,
In juicy wonder, let time pass.

Whispers of the Blooming Grove

In the grove where laughter thrives,
Silly antics fill the lives.
Balancing wobbly fruits so bright,
As giggles burst, what a sight!

Sweet whispers float upon the breeze,
While fruit-spirits hang from trees.
They tease and play, in shades of fun,
A juicy chase has just begun.

With every twist, a funny prank,
Lively joys, a silly tank.
Colors drip from branches high,
With winks and laughs, a merry sky.

Beneath the trees, the stories flow,
Fruitful friendships always grow.
Each playful jest, a bond so true,
In our little grove, we are a crew.

Luminous Citrus Fleeting

In the garden, fruits do dance,
Bright and round, a sunny prance.
They giggle as they catch a ray,
Rolling 'round in a playful way.

Juicy laughter fills the air,
A citrus crew without a care.
Peeled with joy, they find their fun,
Basking bright, each little one.

Bees buzz by, a buzzing cheer,
Kissing fruit, they persevere.
While shadows stretch across the green,
Citrus jokes form quite the scene.

As light fades, the laughter stays,
Fruitful moments, golden rays.
Count the giggles, one by one,
In the garden, oh what fun!

The Sweetness of Sun-Drenched Days

Squeeze a smile, let laughter burst,
Golden rays, oh, how they thirst!
Hidden jokes in each ripe bite,
Giggling in the fading light.

Sweet and tangy, taste the cheer,
Bouncing flavors near and clear.
Juicy jokes spill from my hands,
Shining bright, like bandit plans.

A playful breeze wraps 'round the trees,
Whispering secrets, tickling leaves.
Each little nibble, a funny tease,
Harvest laughter, oh, what a breeze!

As the sun slips down the sky,
Citrus giggles wave goodbye.
A toast to joy, in every way,
Sweetness lingers, come what may!

A Canvas of Zesty Dreams

Splashes of yellow, bursts of cheer,
Life's a canvas, bright and clear.
With every slice, a giggle grows,
Colors bright, as humor flows.

Paint my world with zest and fun,
Laughter rising, one by one.
Juice drips down, a wicked trick,
Peeling laughter, oh so quick!

Dreaming vivid, dreams so bold,
Crack a joke, let joy unfold.
With a wink and a twist of fate,
Citrus cobbler feels just great!

Underneath the painted skies,
Where each fruity laugh defies.
A swirl of laughter, bright as day,
In this orchard, let's all play!

Bright Laughter on the Orchard Breeze

A breeze of giggles through the trees,
Whispers of joy, a playful tease.
Lemon-shaped hats on heads delight,
In this orchard, everything's bright!

Cheeky fruits, they trade their pun,
A citrus chase, oh what a run!
Rolling down the grassy hill,
With every bounce, the world's a thrill.

Squishy jokes and sour strings,
Delicious laughter, goodness brings.
Pineapple crowns, they dance around,
A jolly riot, laughter's found.

As sunsets glow, the giggles swell,
In this orchard, all's quite well.
Raise a toast to fruity cheer,
Underneath, we shed a tear!

Citrus Serenade in the Daylight

In a grove where laughter burst,
Fruits hang low, ready to burst.
They giggle with the breeze so bright,
Tickling bees in morning light.

A parrot squawks with glee so loud,
As squirrels dance beneath the cloud.
Their mischief fills the sunny air,
Citrus jesters everywhere!

A lemon sings a zesty song,
While limey notes tag along.
Orange peels with playful spins,
As laughter rolls and joy begins.

So grab a snack, join the cheer,
In this fruity atmosphere.
With every bite, the sweet delight,
Turns silly smiles and hearts so light.

Sunrise Over Juicy Gold

The dawn arrives with zestful kicks,
A citrus party, full of tricks.
The tangerines do cartwheels bright,
As sunbeams pull away the night.

A grapefruit jokes with cheery zest,
While others nap, it takes a rest.
They tickle each other, juicy fun,
Under this playful, glowing sun.

An orange wears a funny hat,
And dances with a chubby cat.
A merry crew in morning glow,
With every twist, their laughter flows.

Let's toast the day, oh what a sight,
With juice to make our hearts feel light.
In this bright, fruity escapade,
Let's dance along, our silly parade!

Sunlit Citrus Dreams

In fields where laughter fills the air,
Citrus wonders without a care.
A lime rolls down a grassy hill,
As giggles echo, never still.

Beneath the blue, a game begins,
With fruit that plays, everybody wins.
A lemon juggles with delight,
While nectarines hop left and right.

A sunbeam shines upon their face,
While oranges join in the race.
Each juicy splash, a burst of joy,
With every twist, they laugh and toy.

So come and join this fruity fun,
Where happiness is never done.
In sunlit dreams, the fun's not through,
With every laugh, we're born anew!

Radiance of Ripe Fruit

In a garden full of cheeriness,
Ripe fruits twirl with such boldness.
Banana splits with giggling glee,
As berries burst with jubilee.

A swaggering peach starts the dance,
With every wobble, takes a chance.
Cherry pops, a bouncing sprite,
Creating giggles, pure delight.

The tangerines tell silly tales,
Of travels on fruity gales.
With zest and flair, they steal the show,
In this radiant, juicy glow.

So here's to all the silly sights,
And fruity friends on sunny nights.
Join the laughter, feel the thrill,
In this ripe realm, we love the chill!

The Orchard's Embrace

In the garden, fruits do sway,
With laughter, they jump and play.
A bunch of zest, what a delight,
Squeezed and squished, oh what a sight!

The trees wear crowns of dappled hue,
While squirrels conspire, it's true,
With each giggle, fruits start to smile,
Making juice for us in style!

The branches sway, a dance so bright,
Birds chirp jokes, oh what a flight!
We pick the fruits, oh what a race,
With messy hands, a juicy embrace!

So come and feast, let laughter flow,
In this orchard, joy will grow.
With every sip, a hearty cheer,
A sunny smile, the best of years!

Golden Spheres of Light

Round and plump, they glow and tease,
Rolling down, a laugh with ease.
A game of catch beneath the trees,
Chasing fruits that float like breeze!

Splashes here, a juice brigade,
Sticky fingers, oh what a trade!
In the laughter, we find our cue,
A sunny picnic, just me and you.

Whispers shared with every bite,
A citrus burst, pure delight.
Bouncing flavors like a song,
In this fruity game, we belong!

At twilight's end, we can all rest,
Tangled tales, we'll surely jest.
In the light, our giggles stay,
Golden spheres, come out and play!

Juices of a Midsummer Day

On a day so warm and bright,
Fruits tumble down, what a sight!
Juicy drips and slurping sounds,
  Laughter dances all around.

We juggle fruits with silly glee,
Against the tree, let's climb and see.
With splashed sunshine on our chin,
Who knew fruit fights could be such a win?

The ground is sticky, feet all stuck,
A slippery game of silly luck.
Sweetness drips from every bite,
  Underneath this glowing light.

So gather 'round, let's toast away,
To laughter shared, in bright array.
In juicy fun, we'll find our way,
Creating memories this summer day.

Citrus Bliss Beneath the Sky

Beneath a blue, a citrus treat,
With every laugh, we find our beat.
Sliced and splashed in vibrant hues,
Under the sun, we pick and chose.

With juggling fruits, our hands are quick,
Who knew that juice would make us slick?
Fruits like smiles roll round and round,
In this jolly place, joy is found!

Sippin' sunshine from a cup,
Goofy faces as we sup.
With every giggle, we're in sync,
Citrus magic in every drink!

So here's to fun and zestful days,
To laughter shared in silly ways.
With juicy sweetness, life's a ride,
Beneath the sky, it's joy we ride!

Sunkissed Splendor on the Grove

In the grove where laughter sings,
The fruit wears crowns, like little kings.
They bounce around on branches high,
With chubby cheeks, they wave goodbye.

The trees gossip in rustling leaves,
Each whisper telling funny eves.
A squirrel darts, takes aim for fun,
While dodging rays, the dance begun.

Glimmers of Citrus and Sky

A twist of fate, they ponder bright,
As bees in shades of golden light.
With every buzz, a comedy,
In sunshine's glow, they dance with glee.

The birds are jesters, chirping loud,
In leafy costumes, proud and proud.
They sneak a sip of nectar sweet,
While oranges roll beneath their feet.

Warmth of Harvest in Bright Fields

The fields are dressed in vibrant hues,
Where fruit debates the best of views.
They joke about the summer's scheme,
And chase the sun, a fruity dream.

The farmers dance with pitchfork flair,
While veggies plot to steal the air.
Each season's end brings giggles bold,
As laughter warms the sunset gold.

Tasting the Day's Radiance

A taste of sunshine on our lips,
With rays that tickle, gentle quips.
The juice spills forth, a citrus fun,
In every drop, we share the sun.

In picnics bright, we laugh and play,
As clouds parade, they steal the day.
The sweetness bursts in every bite,
A carnival of joy, pure delight.

Radiant Harvest Under Blue Skies

Bright fruits dance on the trees,
Chasing bees in a gentle breeze.
Laughter echoes, kids run around,
A citrus circus right on the ground.

Squeeze a wedge with a silly grin,
Watch the juice drip, it's fun to begin.
Sticky fingers, a zestful show,
Who knew fruit could put on a glow?

With hats so big, we look quite absurd,
But the joy we feel is simply unheard.
Under bright rays, our picnic's a blast,
A feast of laughter, it's ripe and vast.

As we feast on zest and delight,
The day's so perfect, hearts feel light.
In this orchard, we play and sing,
Who knew oranges could make us swing?

Juicy Treasures of the Season

Peeling laughter, zest in the air,
Juicy treasures, we happily share.
A citrus smile from tree to tree,
Nature's candy, wild and free.

Squishy cheeks after each big bite,
Sunshine giggles, oh what a sight!
With each drop of juice, moments burst,
Funny faces, it's all rehearsed.

The juicer's on, what a crazy ride,
Citrus splatter, oh how we glide.
Sipping nectar, we avoid the sting,
In the orchard, we dance and swing.

With funny hats and fruit-filled play,
We'll laugh until the end of the day.
A citrus treasure, a feast so grand,
In this sunny world, we take a stand!

Days of Tangy Delight Await

Sunny mornings, we chase the light,
Tangy wonders, what a bite!
Smiles as bright as the glorious fruit,
Skipping in rhythm, oh how we toot!

Slicing wedges, a madcap spree,
Juice drenching clothes, young and free.
With laughter ringing far and wide,
In each orange, we take great pride.

A fruit fight's on, it's a sticky blast,
Laughing hard as they come flying fast.
We wear our snack, a juicy crown,
In this lovely orchard town!

From tangy jams to fresh-squeezed cheer,
Our days are bright, the fun is here.
With every squeeze and every grin,
The sweet taste of joy just cannot thin!

Sun-Kissed Moments Unfold

Under the rays, we jump and play,
Citrusy laughter leads the way.
Every slice, a spark of fun,
Sticky smiles for everyone.

A fruit parade, we march in line,
Squeezing juice with a wacky sign.
Peeled and plucked, all in a row,
Who knew fruit could steal the show?

With goofy dances and silly cheers,
We wrangle flavors, banish fears.
In sunny patches, our joy is bold,
These moments, like bright treasures, unfold.

With every bite, we share a dream,
In fruit-filled laughter, we brightly beam.
So grab a slice, join the delight,
Under golden skies, everything's right!

Glorious Amber Reflections

In a grove where giggles grow,
Fruit dances in the golden glow.
Tiny critters steal a bite,
While the world is pure delight.

Sunny faces all around,
Lemonade smiles are truly found.
Joking limbs with teasing sways,
Life's a game, a fruity maze.

Bouncing squirrels, juggling cheer,
Flip-flops squeak, oh what a year!
When the rays are bold and bright,
Zesty laughter fills the night.

Juice-stained fingers wave with flair,
In a world with zest to spare.
Every slice, a giggle sound,
In this joy, we've all been crowned.

Sun-Drenched Fragrance of Life

Whispers of zest twirl in the air,
Ticklish breezes without a care.
Playful scents that tease the nose,
Make us dance on our toes.

Jovial bees buzz, always late,
Stealing bites from nature's plate.
With sticky hands and blossomed pride,
We all share laughter as our guide.

Silly hats adorned with fruit,
Everyone's favorite sunny loot.
Giggles spill like juice from trees,
In this warmth, we find our ease.

Smiles shine brighter than the day,
Grins and glee, let's sing hooray!
In this glow, hearts feel so free,
Join the fun, just wait and see!

Vibrant Citrus Moments

Lemon drops and laughter fly,
As we race the clouds up high.
Each slice a story, each peel a joke,
Wrapped in sweetness, life's real poke.

When the sun's laughter fills the sky,
Even the birds seem to fly high.
Chasing shadows with goofy grace,
Fruits and friends, the perfect place.

Witty jabs and fruity puns,
No tired frowns, just silly runs.
Laughter echoes through the trees,
In this sunshine, we feel the breeze.

Each moment bright, a slice to share,
With jokes and smiles floating in air.
So grab your crew, don't take the bus,
Let's savor life, just sit and fuss.

A Tonic of Sunshine and Sweetness

Mixing laughter with a twist,
Flavors bounce and swirl, we insist.
With every sip, we toast and cheer,
To warm hearts and banter near.

Fruit hats bobbing left and right,
Silly dances in the light.
Zesty songs that make you grin,
We all join in, let the fun begin!

Chasing rays as shadows shrink,
With every moment, we pause to wink.
A sparkling splash, a sunny toast,
Filling hearts with joy, we boast.

So gather 'round, embrace the thrill,
This sweet concoction gives us chills.
In a squeeze of love, we find our way,
Under bright skies, we laugh and play.

Burst of Juicy Sunshine

Radiant spheres climb the high trees,
Dancing like clowns in a warm breeze.
Each bite brings laughter, a squirt and a grin,
As juice trickles down, let the fun begin.

Lemonade laughter in the bright rays,
Tangy tales shared in mischievous ways.
A fruit fight erupts, giggles abound,
As sticky fingers paint joy all around.

Sunbeams shine bright on the vibrant feast,
A fruit party started, no way to be ceased.
The sweetness delightful, the moments divine,
Life's fruity circus, oh, how we shine!

With each pulp explosion, we bask in delight,
The taste of pure joy in the glorious light.
We'll caper and twirl, let our laughter explore,
In this zesty playground, who could ask for more?

Citrus Glow in the Evening Air

Evening creeps in with a zany twist,
As citrus shapes dance, they simply insist.
With zest on our lips and giggles galore,
Every slice shared opens new laughter's door.

Candles flicker bright, matching our cheer,
As fruit hats dance, let's spread the good sphere.
The sunset drizzles like sweet tangerines,
As we dash through the grass, weaving silly scenes.

Squeezed in tight laughter, a feast for the soul,
Citrus delight makes us lose all control.
In the warm daylight, our giggles run free,
As we bounce like fruits, just wild as can be!

With each chubby bite, our spirits do lift,
In this golden hour, it's nature's sweet gift.
The glow of the charm, in the evening we share,
Mirthful and bright, like a love affair.

Luminous Edges of Nature's Palette

Colors explode where the sun hits the grove,
An artful design in the land that we rove.
Splash of bright colors in giggly delight,
Nature's own palette, a truly wild sight.

We pick and we laugh, the fruit's our delight,
With each comical slip, our joy takes flight.
The fruits are our canvas beside the sweet stream,
Creating a masterpiece born from a dream.

In sunlit embrace, we play peek and seek,
With laughter weaving magic, we're playful and cheek.
Citrus like chatter drips down from our arms,
Spilling warm wishes and playful charms.

The edges grow luminous, sparkling with cheer,
Each giggle a brushstroke that brightens our sphere.
Together we dance on this color display,
In laughter and sunshine, we joyously play.

The Symphony of Sweetness

In the orchestra found where the zest comes to play,
A symphony rises at the end of the day.
Note after note, as laughter takes flight,
The sweetest of songs begins with delight.

With plucky tomfoolery and citrus on track,
We're dancing in rhythm, no looking back.
Splat of a segment sends giggles around,
As the melody twirls, our antics astound.

The sun plays its tune, strings pulling on smiles,
As the zest of the orchard joins in for miles.
In this fruity concert where fruit hats abound,
Harmony sparkles, pure joy can be found.

So let's raise a toast to this wild little spree,
Where sweetness and laughter flow wild and free.
In this zesty symphony, friends sing along,
In a fruity celebration, let's all be strong!

Nature's Brightest Essence

In gardens where the laughter grows,
With peels that gleam, the fruit bestows.
A slice of joy, the juice it spills,
A giggle blooms in sunny gales.

The bees are buzzing all around,
As fruity scents come tumbling down.
A squirrel slips on a fruity treat,
It's quite the show, oh what a feat!

Citrus Hues in the Daylight

A zesty dance upon the floor,
The yellow blobs we all adore.
They roll and bounce with such delight,
A comical sight in broad daylight.

With every squirt, a giggle grows,
As citrus slips and laughter flows.
Their tangy charm, a wicked scheme,
An orchard's plot, or just a dream?

A Burst of Sunny Flavor

A fruity fling on summer days,
With pucker faces in the rays.
Sweet citrus bombs that zing and cheer,
They bounce around, our fun is near.

An orange cat, he starts to chase,
A bouncing ball, oh what a race!
But in the end, he makes a splash,
Our juicy hero, oh what a bash!

Fields of Gold

In fields of gold, the laughter swells,
A citrus drive with all its bells.
The fruit parade, so bold, so bright,
A funny show, pure delight!

A squirrel's feast, a jester's joke,
As juicy laughter starts to poke.
They tumble down in silly cheer,
Rolling forth with no doubt or fear!

Zest of Life

A little zest for every laugh,
The brightened world is quite the craft.
With every peel, a laughter's bloom,
These fruity wonders start to zoom.

In shades of bright, the joy ignites,
As funny moments take their flights.
We burst with glee, oh what a treat,
In this sweet life, we find our beat!

Sun-Drenched Radiance Unbound

Golden globes hang with cheer,
Nature's laughter rings so clear.
Up they bounce in a playful dance,
Under sunlight, they seize their chance.

Beneath the trees, carefree and bright,
Gathering fruits, what a silly sight!
Juice drips down, a sticky mess,
We giggle loud, our laughter's blessed.

Light beams wink and shadows play,
Chasing dreams, we laugh away.
Silly hats on every head,
Thinking thoughts we'll never shed.

With every squeeze, the juice just flies,
We make funny faces, no surprise.
This fruity world where we belong,
In every bite, we sing our song.

Citrus Poetry on the Horizon

Zesty scents drift in the breeze,
Laughter grows among the trees.
We toss and catch, a citrus game,
Juicy victories, never the same.

The sun's a friend, it's here to play,
Bouncing rounds all through the day.
Giggles echo, bright as can be,
If fruits could speak, oh, what glee!

A quirky dance beneath the shade,
With every sip, our worries fade.
Squeeze the day, it's time to cheer,
In this orchard, all's a dear.

To burst with flavor is our quest,
Tickled by sunshine, feeling blessed.
With every drop, we find pure fun,
The day rolls on, we've just begun.

A Palette of Sunshine and Flavor

Colors splash in a bright array,
Fruits laughing through the warmth of the day.
A rolling ball, it takes a swing,
Who knew nature could be such a thing?

We paint the air with our delight,
Chasing shadows, oh what a sight!
Bubbly brains in a juicy haze,
Time for silly, sunny days.

With zesty bites, we dance around,
Skipping steps, what joy we found.
Each slice brings a grin so wide,
In this sweetness, we all abide.

Witty jests hang in the light,
Flavors mingle, truly a delight.
Together here, we laugh and play,
In this vibrant, sunny ballet.

Morning Glories in the Grove

In the grove, laughter sprouts,
Sunshine's warmth, what it's about.
A dash of fun on each bright face,
Fruits rattle joy in our happy chase.

With each pluck, a giggle grows,
Strange flavors, nobody knows!
Sticky smiles and messy hands,
Playing games on nature's sands.

Sweaty brows and sunshine beams,
This is where we chase our dreams.
We jump and hop, a fruity quest,
In this groove, we're all the best.

Oh, the stories these fruits could tell,
Of silly moments and laughter's swell.
Together we sip, munch, and run,
In this merry land, we have our fun.

Warm Embrace of Citrus Radiance

In a grove where laughter swells,
Round fruits dance like little elves.
With zestful smiles, the branches sway,
Bright hues chase the clouds away.

Squeeze the joy on sunny morns,
Sweet and tangy, no need for scorns.
They slip and slide, a citrus game,
Each bright burst, a giggling flame.

Beneath the boughs, we bounce about,
With sticky hands, there's never doubt.
We juggle life with juicy cheer,
A citrus party, round and near!

When dusk arrives with playful grins,
Our fruity frolic never thins.
We bask in rays, so warm and neat,
Our hearts as bright as every sweet.

The Flavor of Hope in Sunlit Days

Zesty mornings bring a grin,
Peeling laughter from within.
With every bite, we make a scene,
Life's a citrus, fresh and keen.

Sliced creations made for fun,
Squeeze and squirt, we run and run.
A splash of juice, a sip of glee,
Waking joy like a buzzing bee.

In picnic spots where friends unite,
We toss the fruit—what a delight!
A juice-filled jug we proudly pour,
With every laugh, we shout for more!

So grab a slice, don't be shy,
Let citrus love float in the sky.
We'll taste the day, oh what a flair,
With hope as bright as sun-kissed air.

Twilight's Citrus Glow

As the sun dips low, colors spread,
In a citrus world where play is bred.
We twirl and leap, with zestful grins,
Sipping twilight, where fun begins.

Candies of citrus, twinkling bright,
Chasing shadows into the night.
We giggle loud, the stars our stage,
With tangerine tales, we turn the page.

The gloaming glow, like syrupy dreams,
In the orchard, laughter beams.
Each fruit a wish, a playful tease,
As the breezy night brings us ease.

Under starlit skies, we revel and play,
With every sip of our citrus fray.
Joy cascades like moonlit streams,
In twilight's embrace, we chase our dreams.

Splendor of Citrus Dreams Aglow

In morning light, we take our flight,
With citrus dreams, oh what a sight!
Each zesty laugh is bright and bold,
With stories shared, our hearts unfold.

A fruit parade, in colors bright,
Rolling laughter brings pure delight.
We toss and catch, a playful crew,
Juicy moments, all brand new.

When afternoon glows, we gather round,
With minty treats and joy unbound.
Sweet circles dance in every hand,
Creating fun, just like we planned.

As night descends, we still feel light,
With citrus dreams, our spirits ignite.
In those bright colors, we find our way,
Laughter ringing like bright cabaret.

www.ingramcontent.com/pod-product-compliance
Lightning Source LLC
Chambersburg PA
CBHW070309120526
44590CB00017B/2602